Poor

Kathmandu

Interviews with people

living in poverty in Kathmandu

Publisher: Books on Demand GmbH, Copenhagen, Denmark

Print: Books on Demand GmbH, Norderstedt, Germany

ISBN 978-87-7170-157-9

Poor

Kathmandu

Is beauty also in the lifestyle of the poor?

CONTENTS

PREFACE

Kathmandu is a large city occupying around 50 km2, inhabited by around one million people. The surrounding area of the Kathmandu Valley covers an area of almost 560 km2, and is inhabited by almost 3 million people. It's by far the highest concentration of people in the country of Nepal.

It is almost self evident that in one of the poorest countries in the world with such a concentration of people in a relatively small area, not everyone can be well of. There will be areas of slum, there will be beggars, and there will be a lot of low income jobs with very low earnings.

I have tried to locate and map some of these groups to analyse their way of living in trying to find both the most negative and positive sides of their lives. For some it seems hard to find anything else but a struggle to survive but there are bright spots, so bright that the otherwise grave looking faces of these people lighten up when talking to them about these high points of their lives, however few they may be.

Strangely, the people of Kathmandu are on average some of the least poor in Nepal. But, counted in numbers due to the high population concentration, Kathmandu houses a lot of the poor people of Nepal.

What is hard to measure is how the poverty in the rural districts across Nepal is affected by their ability to exploit some of the sourrounding natural resources. This at least is not possible in cities like Kathmandu. Therefore, the effect of the poverty might actually be more pronounced in the cities compared to people living in the land districts maybe farming sometimes illegally some of the sourrounding country.

My interviews with the poor actually shows some grave examples of poverty, where it is sometimes hard to imagine how they actually survive.

Bo Belvedere Christensen, June 2015.

Facts about Nepal

Nepal remains one of the poorest countries in the world, despite some progress, it is placed 157th out of 187 countries listed in the United Nations Development Programme's Human Development Report 2013.

A national living standards survey in 2011 concluded that more than 30 per cent of Nepalese live on less than US$14 per person, per month.

In the rural areas of Nepal live around 80 percent of the population. These people depend on farming for their livelihoods. Food insecurity and poor nutrition are major concerns in these areas, where about half of children under five years of age are undernourished. Furthermore, most rural households have little or no access to primary health care, education, safe drinking water, sanitation or other basics.

Discrimination on the basis of caste has officially been illegal since 1962 but is still widespread especially in the rural areas, where illiteracy is common.

Moreover, Nepal is prone to frequent earthquakes, severe thunderstorms, flooding, landslides, and glacial melting, whose severity is compounded by the effects of climate change.

Poor families are often obliged to send their children to work rather than to school, perpetuating the cycle of poverty. About one quarter of children in Nepal are engaged in some kind of family or wage labour.

Source: IFAD (International Fund for Agricultural Development)

POVERTY IN NEPAL

From the poverty index map it is evident that the highest degree of poverty is found in the remote North Western part of Nepal and along the Western border with Tibet. Here the population depend entirely on farming, but the rainfall is low and the soil of a poor quality.

Map showing the poverty index for the regions of Nepal

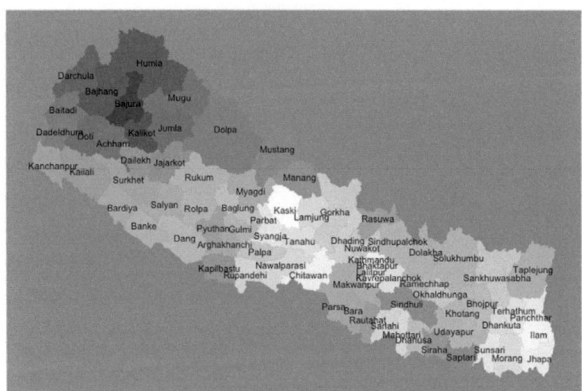

Actually, in this map Kathmandu shows up as one of the least poor parts of the country together with Kaski and Chitwan in Central Nepal and Ilam in the East.

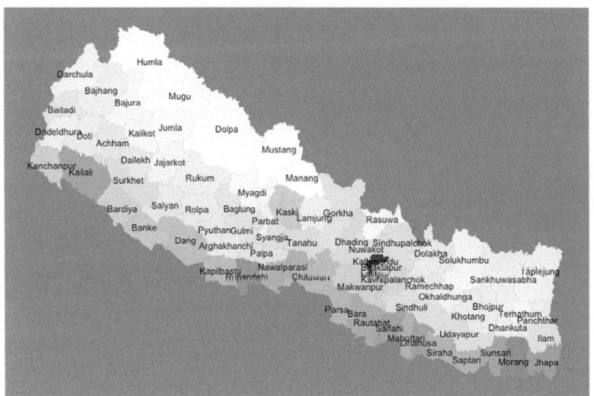

Map showing the population of different regions of Nepal

The distribution of the population troughout Nepal clearly shows the position of the Himalayan mountains.

In the rugged terrain along the border to Tibet few people live and as you travel further south the population density increases. The only exception to this general rule is Kathmandu with its huge population, lying in the middle of the country with respect this general North to South distribution.

The reason for the dense population in the Kathmandu valley was originally the combination of fertile and flat land with a suiting amount of rainfall. Today people move to Kathmandu in hope of getting jobs and the the room for agriculture is decreasing every year. Former small villages on the outskirts of Kathmandu are becoming part of the ever groving population of the capital of Nepal.

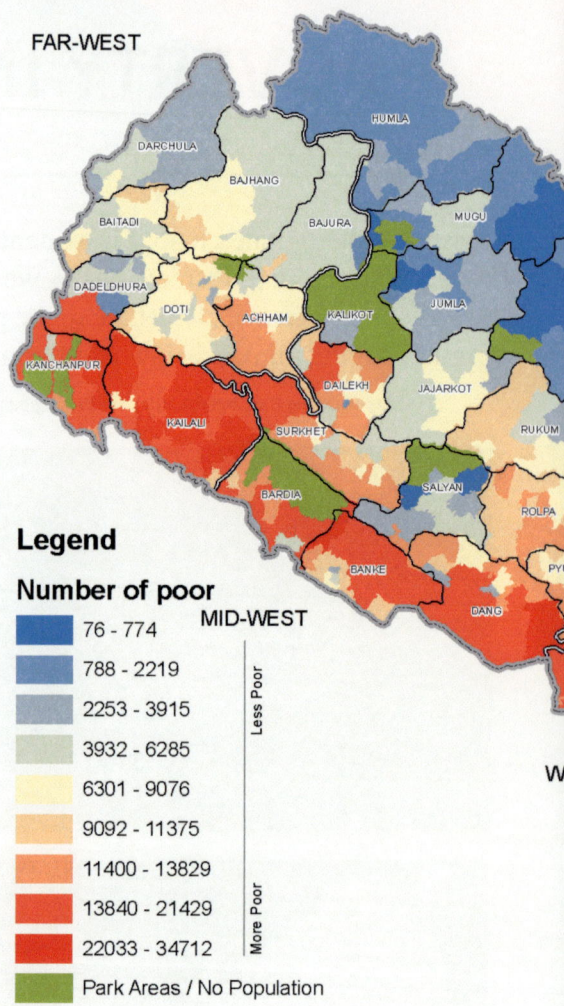

Legend

Number of poor

	76 - 774
	788 - 2219
	2253 - 3915
	3932 - 6285
	6301 - 9076
	9092 - 11375
	11400 - 13829
	13840 - 21429
	22033 - 34712
	Park Areas / No Population

Less Poor

More Poor

Density of poor

Map number of poor per square kilometer and per region shows a completely different picture than the poverty index map. Due to the distribution of the population, the actual number of poor is actually large in in many of those regions where the poverty index is smallest. Kathmandu is on average in this distribution map.

Thus, it is now evident that Kathmandu might not be the most poor part of Nepal, but it is nevertheless a part of Nepal contaning a large number of poor people.

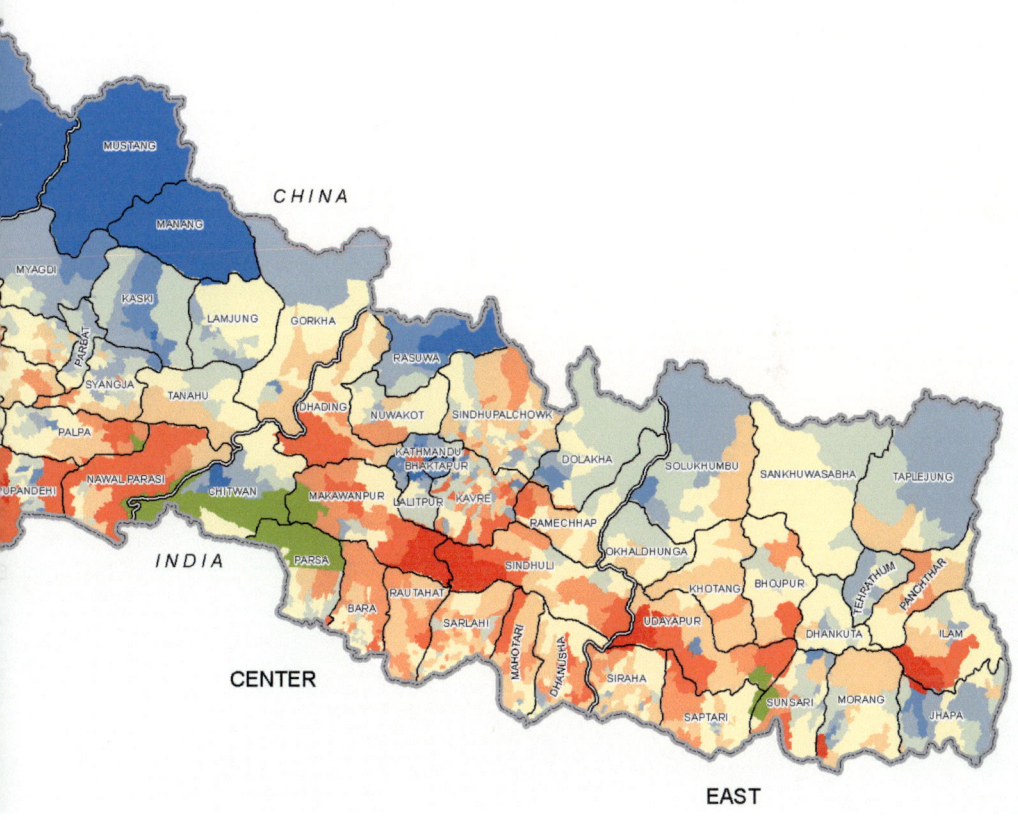

Map showing the number of poor per square kilometer and per region of Nepal

Source: USAID Nepal; data source: World Food Programme, Nepal Office 2010

The earthquake of April 2015 and the weaker earthquake of May 2015 had devastating impact on the capital of Nepal. The effects of this is not clear at the moment of writing, but it will add considerably to the poverty of Kathmandu. Wast living areas were oblitterated, where the people living here are going to stay in the future is not clear. Those who don't have the ressources to rebuild their homes might end up living in the streets and thus add to the poverty of the city.

THE POOR BUT WORKING

Rambahadur, a rickshaw driver

The story of Rambahadur, or Ram as he asks me to call him, is the telling of the life of a rickshaw driver living in Kathmandu since before the town was swarmed by cars, motorcycles and other motorised transportation. Ram is 49 years old.

Ram has worked as rickshaw driver for more than 20 years, living the tourist seasons through in Kathmandu but also part of the rest of the year though business is not so profitable at this time. Totally he's spending more than 8 months in the capital of Nepal every year, time away from most of his family.

20 years ago when he started his work as rickshaw driver, there was more business in town for a guy like Ram. Today the ever-present small taxis have taken over quite a bit of the business.

Rams family of a vife and 4 of his 5 children lives in a small village 90 kilometre outside Kathmandu. In the season Ram doesn't see his family for long periods, working full time in Kathmandu and not returning to his village before the tourists lessen in numbers and the income becomes uncertain. He has a room shared with one of his daughters where he can sleep in the night. His daughter the oldest of his children work in a hotel in Kathmandu. But often in the evenings he rests on his rickshaw in hope of getting a late tourist customer on his way to the hotel from some late opening bar or restaurant.

His wife stays at home at all times, taking care of their small house, "Nepali style primitive" as Ram says. The children, 3 girls and 2 boys, range in age from 13 to 22, the oldest two daughters.

His wife primarily but also Ram when he is home on his seldom visits takes care of a little farming. "Illegal farming, no selling" says Ram and continues, "it's part of the jungle, so we are not allowed to do it." But it

provides the family with some vegetables and thus an important additi-on to the scarce income Ram achieves.

For Ram life is not easy and the economy is uncertain. Outside the tourist season money quickly runs low. Expenses for his large family are high especially when visits to hospitals are necessary. The jungle farm helps them get something to eat, but as soon as money is required it is dif-ficult. In spite of this Ram decided some time ago to send all his children to school and one of his daughters to a college. Though it's a public one, he has to pay for her expenses every day, stay, food, books etc. Not even the public schools have free entry, "I pay admittance fee, and there are monthly payments. Exams have an additional fee," says Ram.

That he actually can afford it although only just makes him feel a little privileged and provides him some comfort in his otherwise poor life. Due to their education, he believes his children will achieve a more rich life and might not live in the same kind of treadmill as Ram.

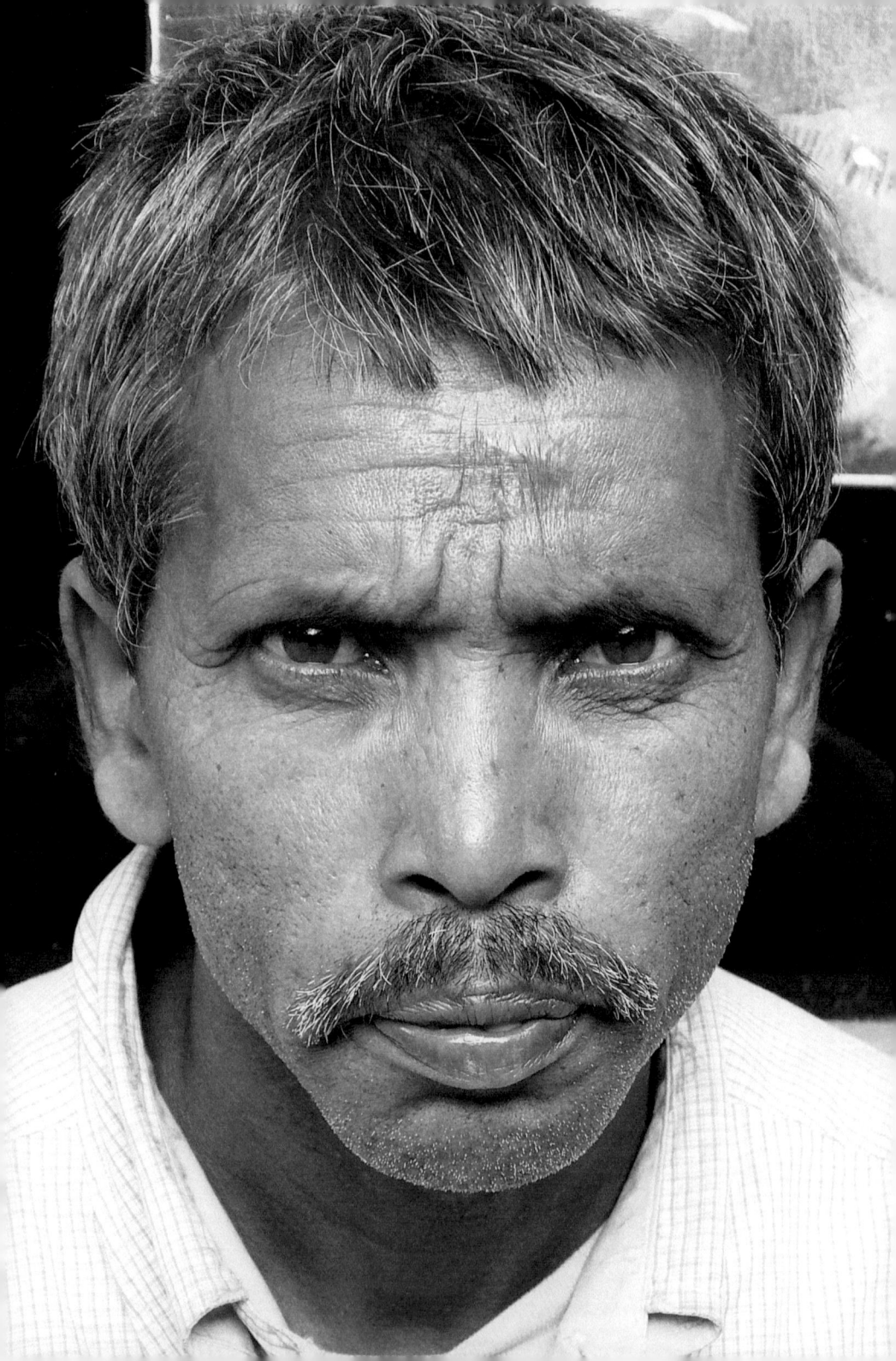

Sanker Das, a street vendor

Sanker is a 48 year old man that has his fixed spot in a sidewalk in Thamel close to Hotel Nirvana Garden and the among travellers famous Everest Steak House. This has been his spot for at least the last 5 years.

His business is his little "supermarket" as his friends jokingly calls it consisting of a small basket with a number of goods like tiger balm, small tourist grade carabiners, penlights, combs, brushes and a number of other things.

He sits tight on this spot day out and day in attracting customers with his little smile, a gesture and maybe a short verbal introduction to his supermarket like "need tiger balm?" or "you want a comb?"

There is no sale and no special offers, but you can always negociate the price with Sanker.

But customers are scarce and there many others like Sanker, many of them selling more aggressively and having a better stand for their "shop." I guess many customers only buy from his basket in pity of his life in the street. But after buying a small thing from him every day for almost fourteen days, I couldn't really think of anything more to buy. Should I then just give him some money, thereby degrading him to a beggar? I couldn't do that, he still has his pride, he has the super market and that is his living.

Sankers home is far from Kathmandu on the border to India, where

---

Facts about Kathmandu: Street vendors

In Kathmandu, thousands earn their living selling goods on streets, sidewalks and in other public places. Due to a steady stream of migrants from rural areas, the number of street vendors grows daily.

Some consider street vendors a nuisance because they obstruct pedestrians and vehicles, however they face considerable obstacles – ranging from expulsion from vending locations to sexual harassment.

According to a research study published in the Pertanika Journal of Social Sciences & Humanities, the municipal government needs to properly manage street vendors by legalizing street vending and providing safe and suitable locations away from busy roads for them to operate their businesses.

The study collected gender-based information on street vendors in Kathmandu, including their income and expenditures, health condition, and the factors that led them toward street vending.

The study found that in most cases, income generation is a secondary role for women but the primary role for men. Both male and female street vendors use their income mainly to provide basic needs for their families.

It is a tough living, street vendors suffer from a variety of health problems, the most common of which are gastritis, headache, back pain, cold and fever.

Source: Asia Research News

most of his family spend their time. He is married and has six children of which the the oldest three - three daughters - are married and doesn't live in their childhood home anymore.

Sanker has 5 brothers that has the same occupation as him, selling from their "supermarkets" in the streets of Kathmandu. Like Sanker their home is far outside Kathmandu close to Sankers home and they have no possibility of spending the night with their family.

Therefore, the brothers share a small room in an old house, where they spend their nights when working in Kathmandu. Sanker and his brothers only visit their home very seldom, at most once in a month, but they spend a lot of time together in the small dark room. Unlike many other occupations depending on the tourists, their business doesn't flourish in the evenings, and they withdraw to their shared night stay relatively early.

Mohan, a fruit vendor

In the streets of Thamel there are several fruit vendors. Either they have an ordinary bicycle equipped with baskets, they have a bicycle with three wheels and a large basket or they have some sort of four wheeled vehicle with a huge carrying capacity.

Mohan who is aged 40 is one of these guys. He has his permanent living in India in an area little visited by tourists, but the business is better in Kathmandu. Therefore, he spends most of his time on the streets in Thamel to sell his fruits to both locals and tourists. I'm immediately offered both orange, banana and fruits I have never before heard of as soon as I see him.

In India he has a full shop, but there isn't many customers. He's wife takes care of the shop while he is here for better income. Almost once every month he travels back to his home just across the border to India. Here he's family awaits his return with money for schools and other bills, that they cannot pay otherwise. He has two sons both of whom are in primary school, and like in Nepal he has to pay a lot of the cost for school.

It is now 15 years since Mohan first time came to Kathmandu and in spite of the four to eight hour long travel to the border depending on the season and the condition of the roads and in spite of the cost of the travel, he will continue to do his major business in Kathmandu.

Without the income from Thamel he wouldn't be able to have his children attend school, and they wouldn't have such a relatively comfortable life as they have. He belongs to the poor, but he actually doesn't feel his life is devoid of pleasures. He have a lot to smile at, his face seldom takes a grave look.

Onreid, a tiger balm seller

Another fellow that you will meet in the streets in Thamel is the tiger balm seller Onreid. He's doing business with a couple of different tiger balm products.

"Tiger balms are good for muscles pains, strained neck, headaches and a lot of other everyday problems," claims Onreid and tries to convince me of the absolute superiority of one of his products. Although, I don't believe it, I can't get it over my mouth to tell him. I end up bying some of his stuff, never to use it.

He has been here in Kathmandu for many years, so many he can't re-member when it actually started. But it is potentially a very long time as Onreid is 58 years old and haven't done anything else but sell tiger balm - all his life.

His home is 55 km outside Kathmandu where his wife lives. He's going back there once in a while, but it is not very often. He has 4 children but they are all adults between 27 and 32 years old. His two daughters are both married an seen to in that way. His two sons both work and live in Kathmandu, one is sewing pants the other is repairing mobile phones. They are living comparatively rich lives - compared to their father and mother.

How they managed to give their children a school time Onreid can't explain, but they did. It would be impossible now with his income, though he's in the same business.

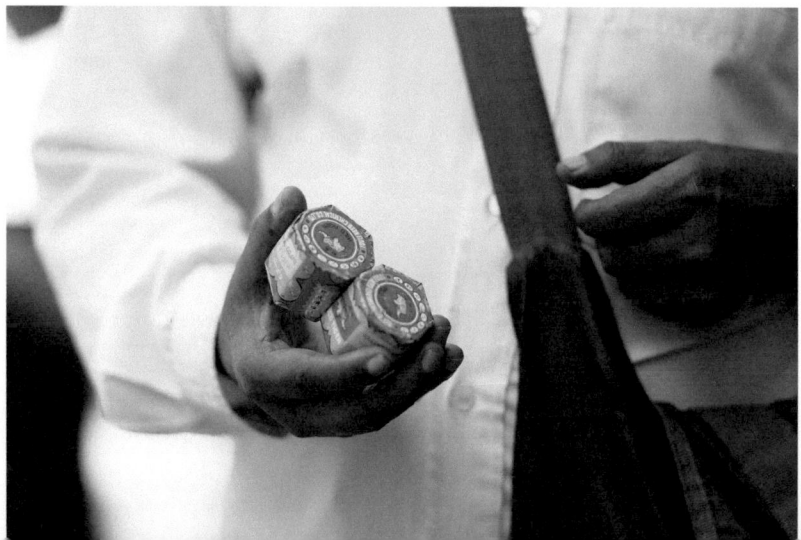

THE EXTREMELY POOR

Raskumari, one of the street beggars

Outside the old Royal Palace, which now a days functions as a public museum, on the pavement sits Raskumari, a 45 year old woman that looks far older than her actual age. She has had and still have a hard life. Luckily her three children are all adults and doesn't need the same attention anymore.

While the Royal Palace was still inhabited by the King of Nepal she was sitting in another part of the town, but after the King had to retire in 2006, she found the street outside the former Royal Palace to be one of the best places for a beggar. Many people pass here, and being close to one of the places with expensive shops, Durbar Marg, it's people from the richer classes that pass her outstretched begging hand.

Raskumari has a home, one rented room, in Kalimaki - one of the slum parts of Kathmandu. She shares the room with her two sons, who have their own lives and incomes although very small. Her oldest child, a daughter, is married and has a low paid teaching job. But anyway all three children are better of than their mother.

Her husband died many years ago when the children were small and the first many years took a large toll on her powers. Even then, she managed to get the children through a basic education, which she didn't have herself. That is one of the few things that can make her smile, that she knows her children will be more fortunate than herself.

> **Facts about Kathmandu beggars:**
>
> There are no reliable estimates as to the number of beggars in the streets of Kathmandu. But we all know them: pity-evoking people in hapless conditions; some blind and some dressed in rags, with unsightly lumps of disfigured flesh for arms and feet; breastfeeding mothers with newborns in their arms, asking for money to buy food for the baby; dirty child beggars with no place to stay but in the streets.
>
> Actually, begging is illegal, the laws preamble portrays it as an act made "to prohibit the tradition of beggary In order to maintain good conduct and morality of general public." It is needles to say that the law has had no impact in reducing beggary.

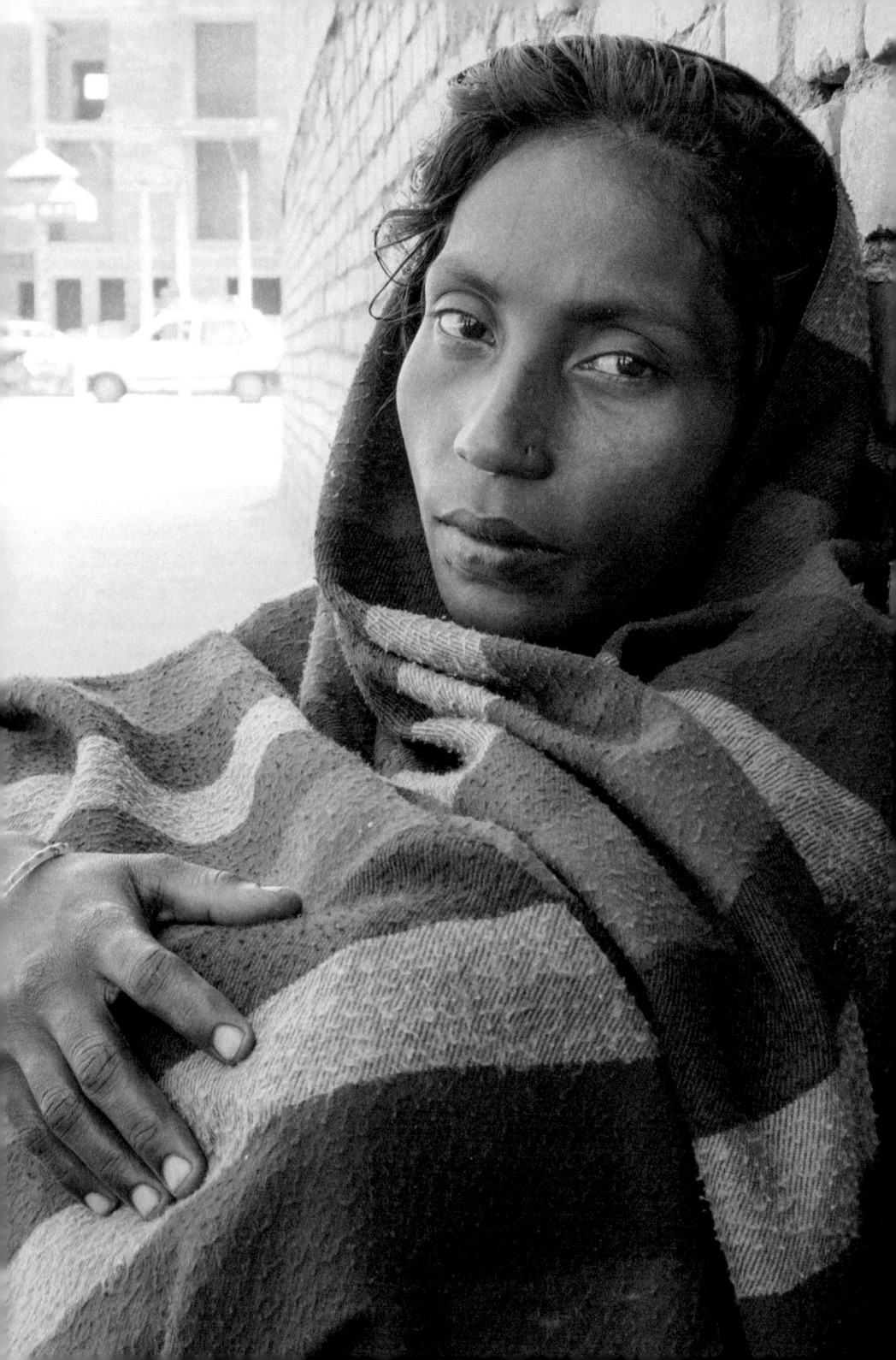

Seidun, another of the street beggars

Almost opposite in the same street as Raskumari sits Seidun with two small children running around her. As soon as I approached Raskumari, Seidun came to the other side of the road to make sure nothing happened to Raskumari. The beggars stick together and take care of each other. When she became aware of my purely friendly attitude, she went back to her own spot, where I saw her sit every day I passed.

When I went to talk to Seidun, the children got hyper active, running around me and doing like their mother, begging with both arms stretched towards me. After having quieted the children with some rupees - though they didn't accept the first small rupee note but knew it had to be bigger to represent some value - they continued their joyful play on the pavement.

Seidun told me her sad story. She was happily married at the age of 22 to a man who although he didn't have a job managed to get money for their necessities. They had three children the oldest of which is now 7 years, and everything seemed just fine. But her husband became bored with her and found a second wife, a very young girl, that he ran of with to India. Although Seidun is now only 30 years and looks quite beautiful, he didn't fancy her and left with the younger wife. To day Seidun has no kind of contact with her husband, doesn't know where he lives and gets no money from him, though they are still married.

Seidun has a single room, that she rents in Doldu, another very poor peoples part of Kathmandu. It is really hard for her to collect enough money for her daily life. She must pay the rent for their room, but she can in no way think about sending the children to school. She could never collect money for the admission fee for her oldest child. And even if she could she wouldn't be able to pay the monthly fee that even the most basic public schools require.

The sad look in her eyes is understandable, there is no light at the end of the tunnel - not for her, and what saddens her most, not for her children. Their fathers leave changed their world completely, no one wants their mother as their wife as she is to old and already have three children. Three chilcren born to become beggars - or even worse, criminals.

A family of beggars

In Tripureswor one of the poorest areas of Kathmandu just behind the town stadium lives a family at the entrance to one of the religious places, Tripura Sundari.

On one side of the entrance they sleep and have their "living room" on the other side is their "kitchen". Here they have a roof above their heads, and close by is a stream of water, not very clean but enough for their purposes. One thing greatly lacking, money for daily necessities.

There seems nothing positive in their live, it's hard to wrench a smile from them, though it happened when I was photographing their home and almost tripled up a step.

The family consists of Sajita, her son Kumar, her sister Sunita, and her

husband Nabin. They all live here and has done so for many years. Kumar has never been to school and the probability that he will go one day is very small.

Their kitchen inventory consists of a stove and a few pots, a dunk to fetch water, a few knives and no-thing more. How they get enough money to buy their food is hard to tell. They are beggars and begging is their only income. They have no money for school, no money to pay for rent, only just enough for the food and that is very basic things like rice, lentils and some vegetables - and they only survive provided they live as they do in the entrance to Tripura Sundari.

Shivanshu, a holy man

When you go to Pashupatinath to see burning of the dead and the distribution of their ashes in the river of Bagmati, you also meet a number of "holy men".

These men seem to live a more gentle life than most beggars of Kathmandu. The men at Pashupatinath receive a fair daily income and seem to lack nothing.

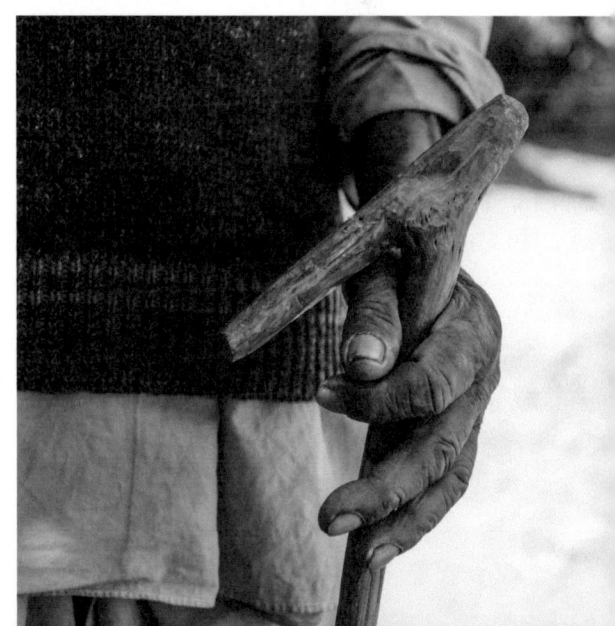

They have easy to smiles, they make practical jokes with the tourists - which I take definitely as a measure of a life that is bearable.

Otherwise hard is the life of the real holy men, that don't do it as a show-up for the tourists. One of these, Shi-

vanshu, live in the Tripureswor area. He is an old man suffering from several diseases, one of which is that he has lost the sight on one eye. Parodoxically, the hospital specialising in eyes lies right besides where he lives. But the hospital is private and only receives paying customers. He had no money for that when he developed a severe infection in his eye. It is now beyond saving and doesn't do him good any more.

He is a beggar like all holy men, but unlike the so called holy men of Pashupatinath his income is very small and he lives a hard and lonely life. He spend a lot of his time meditating, the rest of the time he wanders around the streets of Kathmandu hoping to receive a little money or some food. To him money is not happiness, he just wants to be able to have his daily meal, usually only one and a very simple one.

As a holy man he has no family to support, but on the other hand he's very dependent on his own ability to get the next meal. And no children will help him when he gets to old to wander the streets of the city.

A flower seller on Kantipath

A weight measurer on Kantipath

Driver taking a nap in his rickshaw - this is also the place some of them sleep during the night

Another fruit seller in Thamel

POST SCRIPTUM:

After the powerfull earthquake of April 25th 2015 a lot of homes and other houses in Kathmandu were severely damaged or completely destroyed.

The richer people of Kathmandu lived in tents in their gardens with the prospect of moving into their houses again once the aftershocks faded and the houses had been checked, repaired or rebuilt. Sadly the homes of the poor was hit the hardest, as these houses often were built from cheap materials and without earthquake safe structures.

Many lost their lives in the ruins buried under tons of building materials. Some survived only to live even more miserable lives than before without a place to stay and maybe loosing the few belongings that they had. They have no money to rebuild houses, long time will pass before their lives will be normalised, if that is ever going to happen.

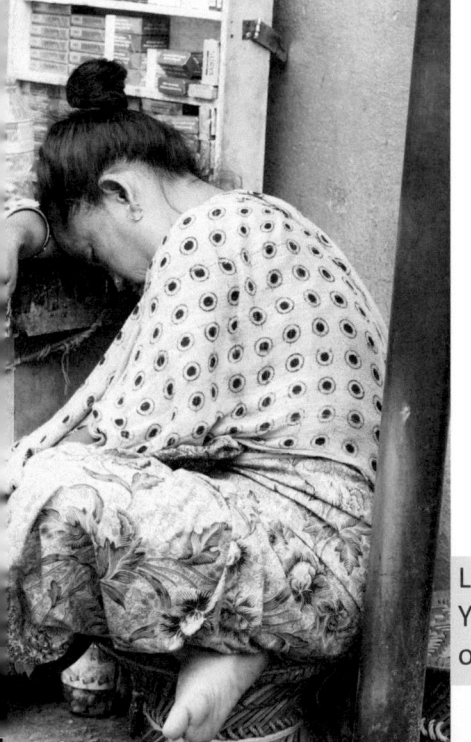

But the reasons to go to Kathmandu and Nepal in general are still there. Though a number of world heritage treasures were destroyed, there is still at lot to see, and some areas are only slightly damaged. Travel to Nepal, spend your money, don't forget the poor, and be happy that your visit helps rebuild the country.

Life is tough also for the shop keepers. You often see them taking a nap while on the job

ABOUT THE AUTHOR

The author of this book, Bo Belvedere Christensen, has visited Kathmandu and Nepal in general more than 20 times. Usually, he comes on expeditions to climb mountains, but through time he has come to know a lot of people especially from the Capital. Many of these are poor people, some of whom live in the streets of Kathmandu.

During a longer than normal stay in Kathmandu Bo decided to start writing a book about these poor people and went around the town together with a Nepalese interpreter as many of the poor doesn't speek anything else but their own tongue. With his camera he spent weeks photodocumenting the lives of the poor and finally he finished this book.

By the same author (most titles in danish):

- Ubetrådte tinder - Gennem hvide pletter på landkortet til toppen af jomfruelige toppe i Himalaya, BoD 2008, ISBN 978-87-7691-358-8
- Big E - Fortællingen om Big E Thrane & Thrane Danish Everest Expedition 2000, BoD 2008, ISBN 978-87-7691-354-0
- Baruntse – over 7000 meter i Himalaya, BoD 2008, ISBN 978-87-7691-953-5
- Baruntse - above 7000 meter in the Himalayas, BoD 2011, ISBN 978-87-7114-250-1
- Vertikalt - Noveller om klatring og bjergbestigning, BoD, ISBN 978-87-7691-477-6
- Klatring i Peru - På udfordrende tinder i Andesbjergene, BoD, ISBN 978-87-7114-206-8
- De Smukke Bjerge - Gasherbrum gruppen i Pakistan, BoD, ISBN 978-87-7114-115-3
- Everest – drømmen og sejren, IP forlag 2000, ISBN 87-90959-02-7, sold directly by the co-author: bbc@k2-adventure.dk
- Ama Dablam – en bestigning af verdens smukkeste bjerg, republishing of the book from 1988 on BoD 2013, ISBN 978-87-7145-635-6
- Mont Blanc - Vejen til toppen af Europa, Gyldendal 2013, ISBN 978-87-0213-381-3
- Kilimanjaro - Guide til natur og bestigning, BoD 2015, ISBN 978-87-7170-165-4